LONDONDERRY

CLANDEBOYE

ARDGLASS

LONGTOWN

NEWCASTLE UPON TYNE
DURHAM
HARTLEPOOL

HEIGHINGTON
HAWES • YORK
HARROGATE
OTLEY • LEEDS
NELSON
LIVERPOOL
MANCHESTER
ALDERLEY EDGE
LINCOLN
CHESTER • CREWE
ASHBOURNE
NEWARK UPON TRENT

NORWICH

DOLGELLAU

BRIDGNORTH
BIRMINGHAM
STRATFORD UPON AVON
WORCESTER
BROADWELL
BOURTON ON THE WATER
BICESTER
STOWE
EASTON NESTON

BECCLES

CAMBRIDGE
SNAPE
WOODBRIDGE

IPSWICH
DEDHAM
LONDON

SEVENOAKS
CHIDDINGSTONE
FORDCOMBE
CANTERBURY
CHARING
MERSHAM LE HATCH
SISSINGHURST
SCOTNEY
RYE
HASTINGS
HERSTMONCEAUX
TELSCOMBE
LEWES
BRIGHTON
HOVE

CARMARTHEN
LLANDEILO
TONYREFAIL

BRISTOL
MALMESBURY
BATH
NORTON ST PHILIP
SALISBURY
MILTON ABBAS
MARLBOROUGH
PETERSFIELD
FARNHAM

TUNBRIDGE WELLS
WADHURST

OXFORD

HOLCOMBE ROGUS
EXETER

POLPERRO

NEWLYN

BRITAIN'S BUILDINGS
PLACES & SPACES

THE UNSEEN IN THE EVERYDAY

Bridgnorth, Shropshire

Local pleasure in an old town, as the tea rooms
building appears to push forward of the pub to
make itself visible from the main crossroads.

BRITAIN'S BUILDINGS
PLACES & SPACES

PTOLEMY DEAN

LONDON NEW YORK MELBOURNE
MUNICH DELHI

To my sister Tacita whose artistry inspired me to draw
throughout our childhood

Editor • Elizabeth Watson

Designer • Vicky Read

Senior Designer • Vanessa Hamilton

Executive Managing Editor • Adèle Hayward

Managing Art Editor • Kat Mead

Production Editor • Luca Frassinetti

Production Controller • Alice Holloway

Art Director • Peter Luff

Publisher • Stephanie Jackson

First published in Great Britain in 2008
by Dorling Kindersley Limited
80 Strand, London, WC2R 0RL

A Penguin Company

2 4 6 8 10 9 7 5 3 1

A CIP catalogue record for this book is available from
The British Library

ISBN: 978-1-4053-2963-7

Printed and bound by Mohn media, Germany

See our complete catalogue at www.dk.com

The English, Scottish, and Welsh places in this book have
been categorized according to their historic (or traditional)
county, rather than their administrative or ceremonial county.
Locations in Northern Ireland have been classified according
to the six counties as specified by the Public Record Office
of Northern Ireland.

Contents

Manchester, Lancashire

Foreword

York, Yorkshire

The river Ouse runs through the centre of York
and cuts an edge through the city, allowing its
density and topography to be appreciated. Drawn
in 1993, the parked cars now have a period charm.

For every hundred who can look, said the poet, only one can see. Ptolemy Dean can see. Such is the introversion of modern British architecture – into a private world of icons and statements, blobs and boxes – that the ideals of context and townscape have all but disappeared. So too has confidence in the language by which Britain's buildings were once described, the language of style, beauty, and proportion.

Into this world Dean steps with a specific mind and a deft pen and brush. He not only takes pleasure in the British picturesque tradition but also has instinct for why millions unacquainted with architectural technique find this tradition so appealing. They like it, quite simply, for being lovely, for expressing the past and present in one visual composition, for diverting the eye and soothing the soul.

Dean understands that no building stands alone, except in a desert. He starts with a lamp post and ends with a signal box, on a voyage that encompasses Britain's streets, squares, mansions, cottages, churches, cathedrals, warehouses even. Each structure forms its impression by sitting in relation to another, then another and another. A house is nothing without its street furniture, its vegetation, and above all its neighbours.

The built landscape is something that both nature and mankind have constantly changed, while merging them into one vision. Size, shape, materials, and colour all contribute to that impression, as does the sense of continuity conveyed by antiquity. They matter, the more so when brought to life by Dean's restlessly wavy line and subtle colour washes.

"It's strange that those we miss the most," wrote Betjeman, "are those we took for granted." Familiar buildings go unnoticed when they are with us, yet are regretted desperately when they are gone – gone when, as Dean says, "we are unable to understand quite why." The task of the artist is to explain why, to draw the eye to a roof line, a perspective, a detail, the shadow of an arch, the tone of brick, wood, and stone. See here, he says, notice and understand. Only thus will we attribute value to the visual feast around us, and know to keep it safe. To this task Dean has brought a delightful talent.

Simon Jenkins

Introduction

This is not a book about architecture. Nor is it really a book about building types. It is more a book about observation, conveyed in the pages of site sketch books accumulated over many years. What the drawings seek to capture is not so much the architecture that surrounds us, but rather the spaces that are formed by it, which create a sense of "place". These are the everyday scenes that we take for granted, often formed by very ordinary and unglamorous buildings.

All too often we look at "buildings" individually and attempt to assess their formal architectural "merit", rather than understanding that their real value may lie in the space that is formed in between them, or through them, or even under them. For example, a collection of apparently hideous corrugated iron structures and sheds can play a vital part in forming a valuable overall composition, such as at the old tannery site in Canterbury (see page 116). This sense of "place" is inevitably hard to illustrate or describe; it may simply be where, for some reason, there is a feeling of comfort or awkwardness. It is an intuitive thing perhaps. Some of us perceive the spaces in between buildings knowingly, but more often than not, unconsciously. It was only when sitting at an outdoor café in Brighton that I looked up and suddenly saw how the sky was shaped and sculpted by the surrounding buildings (see left). It is our interpretation of these subtle elements that shapes our understanding of the character of our towns and villages. This book is therefore a personal survey that seeks to celebrate the places that I happen to have found around me.

The book is organized like a journey, which starts at the simplest of places, in the country. Farm buildings were often gathered to form intimate groupings, such as those at Broadwell (see page 20) or Telscombe (see page 24). Villages are a logical extension of these clusters and invariably create an overall composition of greater value than the individual

Brighton, Sussex

A window of sky shaped by everyday buildings.

buildings themselves. Although originally determined by other factors, the layouts of Heighington (see page 36), Polperro (see page 38), or Bourton-on-the-Water (see page 32) could provide inspiration for the way we plan new housing today.

The book then continues to more sophisticated architectural compositions, such as streets, squares and market places. Streets can be made very enticing, depending on how much thought is given to their visual destination. Town squares are really outdoor rooms, each with four walls and a ceiling that is characterized by the ever-changing colour of the sky. They are utterly unique and we should take greater pride in these places, but all too often they are left awash with cars and marred by atrocious street furniture. The main squares of Beccles (see page 84), Marlborough (see page 76), and Bicester (see page 90) are now basically just car parks.

Our towns have "indoor" spaces too. These range from the simple covered arcade of Dolgellau (see page 94), to the insides of churches and cathedrals, undoubtedly our finest public interiors. Regrettably, the covered railway station at Crewe (see page 104) and Borough Market in London (see page 103) are both threatened with some

Chester, Cheshire

Thomas Harrison's reworking of Chester Castle deliberately framed the composition with a magnificent gateway that dates from 1800 onwards.

degree of demolition. Walls, edges, framed views, and gates all shape our rich urban experience and Chester Castle (see below) is an especially powerful example. Numerous other examples abound, and these should all inspire greater diversity in new design.

The special delight of "townscape" has long been admired, particularly by Gordon Cullen, Edmund Bacon, and Thomas Sharp, whose published work in the 1960s led to an increased awareness of the value of historic towns. Since 1968 there has been legislation to protect places through the designation of "Conservation Areas", but these have proven easy to erode through piecemeal redevelopment over time.

The final sections of the book explore aspects of scale. City skylines are increasingly threatened by new high-rise buildings, for example in Liverpool (see page 194), Ipswich (see page 196), and London (see page 198). While change is inevitable, we can at least notice what is being lost before it goes, even if they are only relatively small delights of detail, like the ornate cast-iron lamps of Hove (see pages 212 to 215) or the toy-train railway signals of Worcester (see page 220). The monster street light in Manchester (see page 5) illustrates how badly things can go wrong.

This collection of sketches seeks to identify what we might not normally see or value; they capture the unseen in the everyday. If vulnerability is a theme of the book, it is only because in our modern, high-speed world we do not always seem to appreciate these places, nor understand the value of the buildings that surround them, and we therefore all too readily just let them go, all in the name of progress. We miss them when they are gone, but are unable to understand quite why.

In new work there is often too much emphasis on the "style" of a building, when really what matters is the way that it sits with its neighbours and how it shapes the "feel" of the place. Until we move away from conventional architectural values and develop ways of recognizing and valuing "place", then much of what has been drawn in this book will remain threatened, and much of what replaces it will continue to lack any sense of human spirit.

Ptolemy Dean.

Wadhurst
Sussex

This collection of drawings starts with no building at all, just a solitary lamp and signpost at the meeting of two country roads (left). The lamp post is a mass-produced nineteenth-century cast-iron column with an early twentieth-century fitting. The shade is inset with pieces of mirror, which resourcefully spread the soft white light of a feeble bulb. The signpost is timber with chamfered sides, an ornate cap, and hand-painted metal letters. The scene (right) occurs nearby at a larger crossroads. As if to celebrate this, the lamp has been given a rather more elaborate mirror canopy, which looks like an upturned frilly dolly. Together, the street lamp and signposts are intimate and humane. They somehow create a sense of place where little otherwise exists, but they are a dying breed in the traffic engineers' world of standardized stainless-steel fittings and orange sodium lighting. Already, since making the drawing, the lamp on the left has been ripped out, and the creeping process of banality has begun.

Ardglass
County Down

Thousands of these single-storey farmsteads were built across the land over the centuries, particularly in Ireland, Wales, and Scotland. Building in a simple row was inexpensive as the division walls between buildings could be shared. Here, the farmhouse has sash windows with cheerful blue frames and rough stone walls with layers of limewash that have softened its texture. The stable next door is more rudimentary. It may once have been thatched to save the cost of slate, but has now been roofed with corrugated iron. The stonework is rougher and the openings are cruder. The corrugated iron, at one time painted red, is quickly rusting to match the colour of the unpainted iron roof on the most basic building on the far right. As the electricity wires do not seem to serve these buildings, it is easy to understand why people might prefer modern bungalows, with all their up-to-date convenience. But these newer buildings are all too often set back behind high leylandii hedges and located at the end of asphalt drives. They create none of the sense of place that these old farmsteads somehow do. Presumably, the mini postbox on the far right will go when the decaying building is deemed too great a health and safety risk for the people collecting the post.

Cousley Wood
Sussex

When is a house a barn or when is a barn a house? This single building is both barn and house, and what is so enjoyable is that we can so easily tell which part is which. The house element is clear to see on the left, with windows, a large stone chimneystack, and neat red brick and tile-hung walls. These tiles hang down like fish scales. The barn section of the building is formed of simple tarred weatherboard and has a large entrance for hay carts with characteristic full-height boarded doors. The choice of these materials expresses a hierarchy of sensible cost restraint – wood for animals, masonry for humans. What is so unusual about this building is the single roof that unites the two. It is rather like an architectural metamorphosis of a caterpillar turning into a butterfly.

Mersham-le-Hatch
Kent

The placing of these two buildings next to and perpendicular to each other conveys a certain intuitive brilliance that is often found in the arrangement of country buildings. Here we can immediately see how the value of the space formed by these two buildings is greater than if the buildings had been constructed further apart or in a line. A further pleasure comes when it is noticed that the scale of the house (left) is matched by the volume of the supposedly subservient barn (right), both of which are swathed by clay tiled roofing that has not yet been uninterrupted by roof windows. Indeed, it is only the number of windows on the house and the large cart loading bay porch on the barn that distinguish the function of these two otherwise similar buildings. We must pray that this barn does not suffer a scheme of residential conversion that would spoil this subtle distinction.

Broadwell
Gloucestershire

The first sparks of spatial energy emerge when more than one building is placed next to another to form a simple farmstead. Here in the Cotswolds, stone barns cluster and gather around farmhouses to create and enclose farmyards. There was no sentimentality here; working buildings were built from the local stone and were placed where they were needed, along natural boundaries, without wasting valuable farmland. They must also have been arranged so as to enhance the defence and security of the livestock from predators both human and wild. With their simple rubblestone walls and utilitarian openings, they are undeniably attractive and despite all our clever computers and practical right angles, groupings of buildings as attractive as these are very hard to reproduce now.

Penshurst
Kent

Having just said on the previous page that authentic
gatherings of farm buildings are hard to reproduce, the
late nineteenth-century architect George Devey certainly
came close to recreating the romantic and picturesque
flavour of them. This collection of farmhouse, barn, and
outhouses was designed to convey an instant sense of the
venerable and the ancient. Devey has indulged in
assembling aspects for a particularly rich form of visual
pleasure. Take, for instance, those mad but splendid stone
chimneys, as if a manor house had been downgraded to
a lowly farmstead. Or the barn, with its jolly half-timbered
porch and dormer windows, perhaps a former banqueting
house? Although conceived as a single composition, an
imaginary history has been threaded through the
architecture of these buildings to suggest a story line
we can but imagine. Despite these domestic and highly
romanticized touches, these buildings still read clearly as
farm buildings. Above all, they are fun, and a refreshing
relief from the joyless approach that is characteristic of
all too many of today's farm building conversions.

Telscombe
Sussex

Sometimes country buildings can find themselves absorbed into villages. Telscombe is an isolated hamlet on the South Downs near Newhaven, where flint is the dominant material. The houses stop where the lane peters into a rough farm track, with a cluster of barns and outbuildings, which screen the empty countryside beyond. The end of the village is crisply marked by the placing of its red telephone box next to one of these barns, reading symbolically as a "full stop" to one type of place and the beginning of the rural world that lies beyond.

Plockton
Inverness-shire

Once houses begin to multiply and to cluster, streets emerge and buildings really begin to exceed their individual worth. This street consists of a typical type of country farmhouse of the simple form that we found in Northern Ireland (see page 14). Here, it has multiplied and evolved into a row along the edge of the harbour. Each house is different in detail, but most conform to a pattern of traditional construction, with roofs of local slate and rough masonry walls, often rendered and limewashed to protect against the weather. It is no surprise that village houses would be like farmhouses, as they were constrained by the materials available locally. Windows and doors could only be as wide as the length of the timber lintels available to support the openings. It is this that defines the architecture of these places and creates regional character. I also liked the line of trees behind the village, which appears to complement the layout of the village itself.

Dedham
Essex

Villages often consist of a row of buildings in a single street, such as here in Dedham, Essex, where the street broadens and curves to catch the south-facing daylight. Dedham was rich from the Middle Ages onwards, and there is a more complex pattern of different building types and materials. There is a timber-framed building in the middle distance, which looks to be the oldest, but is probably no older than any of the other buildings, whose lower roofs and original fronts are now hidden by taller and later Georgian brick façades. Happily, Dedham's wealth mostly only extended to re-facing existing buildings, rather than complete reconstructions. Particularly flashy is the elaborate brick frontage in the centre, built c.1735, whose decorative cornices and pediment were no doubt designed to compensate for its relatively narrow width. The dormer windows and roof of the original house can be seen immediately behind its parapet.

Milton Abbas
Dorset

Detached houses in rows are rarely so picturesque as these cottages of
Milton Abbas, built at the end of the eighteenth century to rehouse
estate workers. The landowner deliberately wanted it to look charming
from afar, so the cottages were thatched and each was made symmetrical.
Not so very delightful for the residents were those cottages that were
divided into four separate and very small flats. Once again, the key to
the visual success of the overall plan was a gentle curve of the village
street, which followed the lie of the land and enabled the cottages to be
seen as a group. The wide lawns in front are unfenced and unplanted
to create a generous open area from which the whole village benefits.
It would be hard to stipulate such control these days, and the spectre
of boarded fences, garden gates, and high hedges can all too easily be
imagined. While privacy for residents would be achieved, all the views
would be blocked and the overall architectural form would be hidden.
Here would be the beginnings of a reclusive suburbia.

Bourton-on-the-Water
Gloucestershire

Bourton-on-the-Water consists of a wide village street, which was unusually built either side of a stream. Like the farmyards of Broadwell (see page 20), the arrangement grew out of functional needs. The street follows ancient paths and the open area accommodated livestock. The prettiness of this (now very chi-chi) village is achieved by the way that the buildings have been pushed back, presumably to reduce the risk of flooding. The buildings all benefit from the deliciously honey-coloured local limestone, and are separated from their neighbours by a space only sufficient for a passing mule or cart. Nowadays the turning circles of fire engines and dustbin lorries appear to determine most new housing layouts. This may maintain safety and hygiene, but inevitably means the loss of enclosure and intimacy.

Hawes
Yorkshire

Hawes is a northern English equivalent of Bourton-on-the-Water (seen on the previous page), but with immediate differences caused by geology. Here the harsher climate and landscape of the Yorshire Dales has produced a fast-running rocky stream, alongside which the houses have clustered. The local moorstone is a rougher building material, but splits well for making large roof slates, and therefore allow the roofs to be constructed at a more shallow pitch. The close proximity of the houses contrasts with the lonely hillsides beyond, and creates a sense of intimacy and homeliness at Hawes, a perception which the traditional red telephone box, with its connections to the outside world, only enhances.

DAMAGE TO THE
VILLAGE GREENS
IS AN OFFENCE
LIABLE TO PROSECUTION
BY THE PARISH COUNCIL

Heighington
County Durham

The need for defence shaped Heighington, County Durham, where standard rows of village houses were arranged as an unbroken, inhabited wall, creating a protected village green at the centre, where livestock could be kept away from potential thieves. This is a wonderful concept as it is the collective value of the individual buildings that forms a giant outdoor space for the benefit of the whole village. As at Milton Abbas (see page 30), the absence of fencing and hedging provides each of the houses with an immediate visual relationship both with each other and with the village green, which is self-policed as a result. Everything seems to happen on this village green: bonfire night, children's football, teenage recreation, and it is complete with a lock-up (left) for detaining those who misbehave – alas, now disused. Although originally designed for very different reasons, Heighington could provide a model of how new villages might be developed in the future.

Polperro
Cornwall

Defence also determined the form of Polperro, Cornwall, where the livelihood of the occupants was fishing. There was not the need to protect livestock from attack as at Heighington (seen on the previous page); rather more the need to protect fishing boats from the weather. In a way, the role of the village green has been replaced by the harbour, overlooked by the tightly packed rows of houses. These houses, each one in itself quite ordinary, collectively create a sense of intimacy and security that contrasts with the wild ocean that lies beyond.

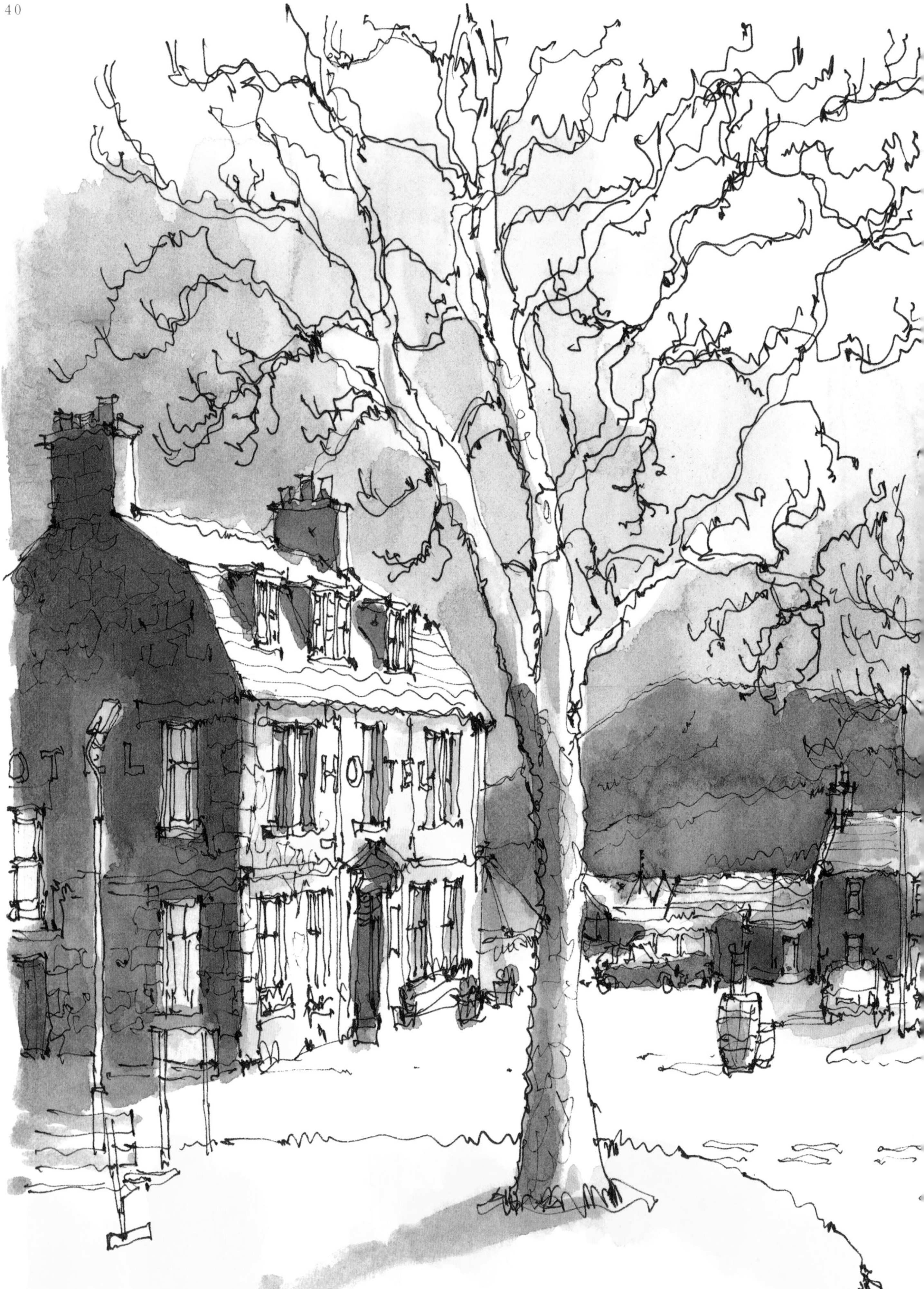
HOTEL
OT L

Archiestown
Morayshire

Archiestown is typical of the small planned villages created in the Scottish Highlands during the eighteenth and nineteenth centuries. It consists of a simple village green with a war memorial at its centre, a small hotel on one side, a church (out of view, behind), and a small collection of houses. The road into the village stretches out dead straight towards the bare mountains beyond; not a place to run out of petrol. While the buildings are fairly widely spaced, there is still just enough building to induce that sense of enclosure around the green, which again benefits from open lawns that belong to all. The loss of any one of these key buildings could diminish the sense of this composition, with a resulting loss of place.

42

Stratford-upon-Avon
Warwickshire

So far on this journey we have seen how simple, individual country buildings gather to create qualities of place, and how when multiplied further, they determine the distinct pattern and character of villages. Towns – the next rung up the urban ladder – develop a more sophisticated application of these basic sensations of place. The main street of an average historic market town shows a unique unfolding drama of "serial townscape". Events emerge and become visible as the visitor passes through them. They are each remarkable achievements, even those shattered by modern redevelopment. At Stratford-upon-Avon, the visual sequence of the high street – one of the best preserved – is captured at a glance. First, there is a wall of jettied timber-framed buildings out of which projects the classical town hall of 1767 – the only building allowed to break the street line. This building is also of stone, asserting its importance further still. Then, at the end, sits a guild chapel, also of stone, and whose medieval tower perfectly terminates the street. Serendipity must have played a role to achieve some of this, but who, I wonder, devised that most gentle but brilliant curve, which as at Dedham (see page 28), allows the whole composition to be appreciated in a single glance?

A sense of town

Kirkwall
Orkney

The main street of Kirkwall on the Isle of Orkney connects its cathedral to the harbour. The street begins wide, with the green of the cathedral yard just visible to the right, but then funnels down unevenly, as the houses along it progressively step forward, framing a distant view of the gentle curve of the main thoroughfare. Unlike at Stratford-upon-Avon (seen on the previous page), there is no clear view of what lies beyond, inducing a sense of mystery that somehow encourages you to move towards it. With a townscape like this, Kirkwall brings out a childhood desire to explore.

Exeter
Devon

At Fore Street in Exeter, the old street from the river bridge is dead
straight and rises uphill to the top of the town where the cathedral is
located. The cathedral cannot yet be seen, and looking up this street,
the view appears long and daunting. There is no enticing vista at the end,
just a row of ugly motorway-style street lamps and the scars of demolition
where the modern ring road now carves its way through at a lower level.

Lewes
Sussex

In contrast to poor old battered Exeter, Lewes
High Street, with its gentle curve, feels much
more appealing. This is partly because the view
is downhill, and partly because the street lights
are better designed, but mainly because the South
Downs rise and enclose the street vista so handsomely.

Salisbury
Wiltshire

Salisbury is dominated by its cathedral, which rises up above the town's buildings, often quite unexpectedly. In contrast to Fore Street in Exeter (seen on the previous page), here on the high street, the cathedral spire and parts of its nave almost glide across the view like a vast ocean liner in a harbour beyond. The relationship between the cathedral and street appears quite unplanned and almost chaotic, but is all the more enticing for it. It is certainly clear in which direction you should walk in to reach the cathedral.

Norwich
Norfolk

In Norwich, St Andrews Street divides in two, with both vistas closed by two towers of the city's plentiful parish churches. Whether this has occurred by chance or good fortune, it leaves us positively spoiled for choice. Both Salisbury and Norwich make the point that our townscape could be much enriched if more thought was given to the potential for views at the end of our streets.

Cromarty
Ross-shire

Bank Street in Cromarty is a planned composition that starts off wide and open to the sea, and then narrows down in three stages to focus a long view onto the pedimented building at the very end. An ornamental column rises above this with the bare hillside beyond. While the buildings on either side are not symmetrical, each one features a window that is strategically placed to allow views down the widened street towards the sea. Once again, ordinary houses collectively create an urban composition of greater value.

Oxford
Oxfordshire

Oxford benefits from the same belt of honey-coloured limestone that serves Bourton-on-the-Water so well (see page 32). Here the stone is cut with a smooth finish to form what is termed "ashlar". This creates a crisp finish to the architecture, which feels more urban as a result. Beaumont Street was laid out in 1828 and was arranged to direct a view straight onto the pedimented eighteenth-century façade of Worcester College. This must have been the plan. But the plan has surely been exceeded. When the college door is left open, a tantalizing keyhole glimpse of the lush, green, and (alas) private gardens is provided down the whole length of the street. Has there ever been a more enticing invitation to trespass?

Bath
Somerset

A sense of urban "layering" is created when buildings and streets occur in differing plains in perspective. On Stall Street in Bath, the building at the centre divides the street into two. Both streets beckon further exploration and convey the three-dimensional complexity of urban space.

Otley
Yorkshire

Layered views are a delight of small and incidental side streets,
as this glimpse of Otley shows. Here, an alleyway forms a useful
short cut between the two principle streets in the town. The path
passes under one building and under another beyond. It's an
everyday scene, but this sort of visually rich townscape would be
impossible to recreate authentically now, which suggests that we
should strive hard to protect it.

Kirkwall
Orkney

We return to Kirkwall (see page 44), to an image that illustrates how lighting at night can enhance the effects of layered views. The main street on the right leads to the darkness of the sea, but the alleyway on the left is dramatically floodlit at its end, and so appears enticing. The lighting draws attention to the curved paving pattern of the road, but leaves the silhouettes of the buildings in darkness. Without a car in sight, it looks like a stage set, complete with a romantically lit phone booth.

Farnham
Surrey

The cobbled surface of Middle Church Lane is dramatically defined by the shadows of the buildings alongside. The view here is also framed by a simple lamp on a bracket, just the type of subtle but enriching layer more townscape views should be given.

Hastings
Sussex

The final layered view in this section of town vistas is at Pelham Crescent in Hastings, an elegant sea-front composition constructed in 1824–28. With one side open to the sea, the framing of the view is achieved by another cast-iron lamp standard (as at Farnham, seen on the previous page) and also the old street railings, whose curved cross bar appears to intercept with the gentle curved parapet of the crescent beyond. The value of railings and lamps in framing views should never be underestimated, and as here, their design should be considered as an opportunity for visual enrichment rather than mere functional banality.

Llandeilo
Carmarthenshire

While it may seem obvious, many ordinary places
are dramatized by topography, which can suddenly
provide new and unexpected views through
buildings or groups of buildings. The lie of the land
is not something that we can generally control, but
we can make the most of it, and often with very
rewarding effects. At Llandeilo in mid-Wales, the
whole layout of the town is immediately apparent as
you enter from the hills above. This is entirely
accidental, but it does provide an understanding of
the urban structure of the town in a single glance.

Norton St Philip
Somerset

The ancient coaching inn at Norton St Philip, Somerset, appears to loom at twice its natural height due to a fall in ground level, which emphasizes its prime hill-summit position. The way that the street beyond is laid out at an angle and diminishes behind the horizon only further conveys the sense that this site is the heart of the place, which was no doubt exactly what the original builders intended.

Edinburgh
Midlothian

The dramatic topography of Edinburgh's Old Town effectively stacks the buildings one on top of another in perspective, creating a wonderfully rich urban cascade. All of this is exploited by the rooftop detail of the individual buildings themselves.

Glasgow
Lanarkshire

Large parts of central Glasgow were laid out on a standard grid-plan in the nineteenth century. In places the grid covers some very hilly ground and crosses it almost unflinchingly, giving rise to some very steep streets and unexpected views. The dramatic topography was exaggerated by Charles Rennie Mackintosh in his design for the celebrated Glasgow School of Art (right), completed in 1907. "Grecian Buildings", to the left, was designed by the equally fine architect Alexander "Greek" Thomson in 1865, and provides the perfect horizontal foil against which the vertical drama of the art school could be played.

Tonyrefail
Glamorgan

In some areas, it seems that the topography of a place was simply a bore that had to be overcome. The functional need for housing industrial workers in the steep valleys of South Wales produced terraced houses that were built hurriedly and inexpensively in the local brick and stone. The lines of the roofs were built parallel to the land below, presumably as one long sloping roof would be cheaper to build than a stepped roof with separate party walls. The resulting buildings, which proudly bear the date 1889, have a character that is undeniably rooted to the unique topography of this place.

Nelson
Lancashire

As at Tonyrefail (seen on the previous page), the streets of stone-built mill-workers' houses march up and down the valley sides of Nelson, Lancashire, but are seen here boarded up for demolition. And yet, as I drew these streets, they were alive with local children playing safely and happily, in what is effectively one enormous sloping playground. Each of the houses appears to have been customized with different paint colours. While probably unintended, the glimpses of parallel streets seen between the ends of the houses provide an attractive sense of layering. I felt that with the necessary modernization, this part of Nelson could have continued to provide accommodation for a stable and humane community.

Bath
Somerset

In eighteenth- and early nineteenth-century Bath, the effects of topography were imaginatively exploited. The valley sides that enclose the city are very precipitous and consequently must have been quite challenging to develop. Close to the top is Somerset Place (left), constructed from 1780 onwards, where the steeply falling ground appears to exaggerate the height of the buildings. As a result, the gracious curve of the crescent rises up dramatically to scoop and embrace the sky. The determination to succeed over the challenges of topography is somehow summed up by the remarkable cornices of St Mary's Buildings (right), by architect John Pinch the Elder (c.1820), which swoop up the hill in a positively baroque spirit. Certainly there is no precedent in the classical world that suggested that cornices could be made as inventive as this.

Edinburgh
Midlothian

Nowhere is the architectural potential offered by topography better celebrated than in Edinburgh. The New Town, developed in the eighteenth century onwards, extends down a north-facing slope with handsome distant views to the Firth of Forth. This remarkable topography was then harnessed and deliberately exploited by an imaginative urban layout. The streets are cupped and curved to and fro to afford a succession of glimpses through open squares to the landscape beyond. And, by chance, this view has come to be perfectly framed by a cast-iron street lamp, with its Scottish thistle bracket. Unpainted and vulnerable, this lamp should be accorded the same protection as the street it illuminates.

Marlborough
Wiltshire

Many of the drawings so far have been concerned with differing types of
street view. But at a certain moment, streets widen and become "squares".
"Square" is an imprecise word and is difficult to define as most of these places
are not square in the formal geometric sense. They are more like large
public outside spaces, utilized for the assembly of people and markets.
Most towns have these squares and their form is infinitely varied. How they
are shaped is determined by factors ranging from geology to defence, rather
like the village greens of Bourton-on-the-Water and Heighington (see pages
32 and 36). In contrast to Stratford-upon-Avon (see page 42), where the
view is most definitely a street, Marlborough's high street feels more like a
square. The town hall, church tower, and two houses form a definite end
in the distance. This composition achieves enclosure, the key ingredient of
any square. It is, in effect, a giant outdoor room for the whole town to enjoy.

The outdoor room

Lerwick
Shetland

The main square at Lerwick has been compressed to its absolute minimum size, and seems heavily protected by the encroaching buildings that surround it. Defence against a harsh climate is paramount, and the placing of the buildings gable-end to the street has increased the number of houses that can be given frontage to the square. The stone-based street lamp provides the perfect urban focus to the space.

Petersfield
Hampshire

While generalization is always dangerous, fundamentally,
squares do require a sense of enclosure. Long open
views out can somehow feel like an unclosed door in a
draughty room. In Petersfield, there appears to be a
visual "draught" as two streets leave the marketplace on
one side (although perspective closes the view of the left-
hand street). The scene is saved by the stately stone war
memorial, which has somehow anchored the place and
provided it with a sense of focus.

Islington
London

This view shows the effect of two "open doors" in sequence across a square. Canonbury Square in Islington is enclosed by terraces of handsome, stock brick, early nineteenth-century town houses, typical of this part of north London. But in this view looking into, and then out of, the square, the street appears to pass right through, creating a howling sense of "visual draught". Conversely, the clear view behind the traffic light, achieved by steeply falling ground beyond, serves to enhance the sense of contrast between the reassuring sense of "enclosure" within the square, and the open outside world that lies beyond it.

Beccles
Suffolk

The Old Market of Beccles characterizes how we tend to treat our open squares today. This area is now used for the turning of buses, for whose passengers two rather utilitarian waiting room structures have been provided. Standard highway engineer street lights on concrete posts have been introduced which are higher than, and consequently diminish the scale of the historic buildings that surround the square. There are large letter markings and double yellow lines daubed across the surface of the road. The ubiquitous plastic traffic bollard neatly summarizes how economy and traffic engineering have been allowed to prevail at the expense of an otherwise delightful urban composition. If this is an urban outdoor room, shared by all of us, then we ought to furnish it with the care and quality that it deserves.

Woodbridge
Suffolk

While the bus stops of Beccles might be improved upon (seen on the previous page), there is no doubt that some of the larger "outside rooms" do benefit from some "furnishing". Take, for instance, Woodbridge, where the square accommodates a very handsome town hall. This sixteenth-century red-brick building is perfectly placed at the narrow end of the square, where it shields the view of the larger, and wider, part of the square beyond, and still allows the geometry of the whole square to be appreciated.

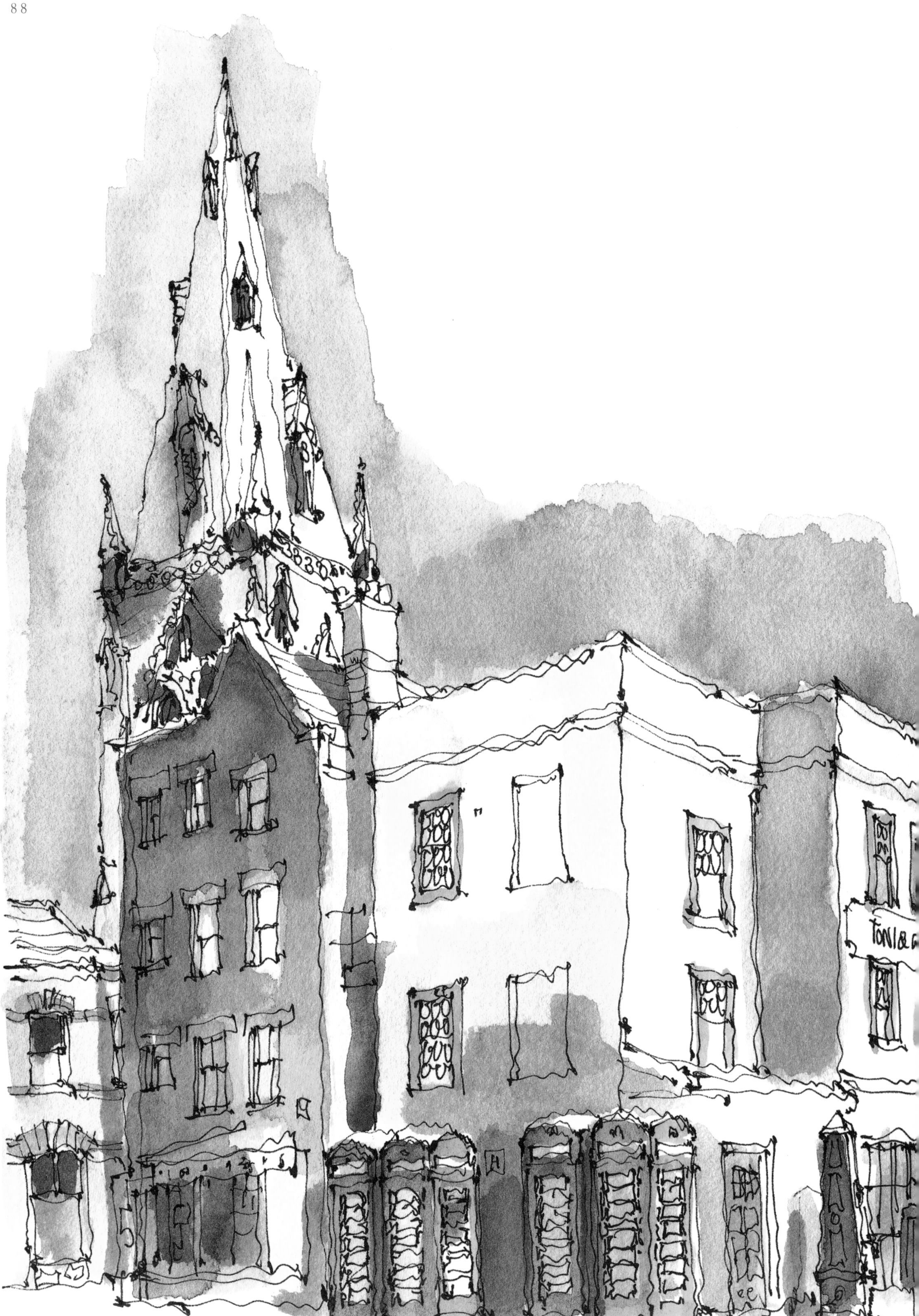

Newark-on-Trent
Nottinghamshire

Newark-on-Trent has a very generous central marketplace that provides a wonderful public space in the heart of the town. Over time, an island of buildings has somehow developed in one corner. Why these buildings were allowed to encroach on the square is not immediately clear but, by providing contrast with the large open area of the rest of the space, they effectively enhance the perceived sense of scale to the square overall. As at Woodbridge (seen on the previous page), we can still appreciate the full size of the space, and these buildings, with the telephone boxes and water pump in front of them, provide a further layer that enriches the view overall.

Bicester
Oxfordshire

Here we see a more advanced state of encroachment than at Newark-on-Trent (seen on the previous page), where the open form of the square has almost become lost due to the number of buildings that have crept into the space. We can still just about determine the overall shape, but only in the glimpses between the island buildings. Although layered views can still be enjoyed around these buildings, they fill the widest section of the square, leaving its smaller end, nearest us, as "left over space," used mostly for car parking. With the backs of the buildings exposed to what is left of this square, the street beyond has apparently triumphed over the square, which appears to have become something of a backwater.

Cambridge
Cambridgeshire

Ultimately a square ceases to be a square when
the building that sits within it becomes so large
that all that is left is the space around the margins,
as here with the Peterhouse College Chapel of
1628–32. The covered arcade linkages to the
buildings on either side introduce a sense that
the outside space is beginning to become an
indoor one. It also suggests that a half-forbidden
and private world lies beyond it, which somehow
entices the visitor to want to proceed towards it.

Dolgellau
Merioneth

Covered public spaces are always an enriching experience in towns. They offer protection from the elements and introduce a welcome sense of enclosure. Street arcades, such as this one in Dolgellau, must certainly be valuable in the rain, but the prime motivation was probably to exploit the full width of the building plot at first floor level above.

CALOGR IORIS
RAS FYNYDD.

The indoor room

Malmesbury
Wiltshire

A number of ancient market crosses survive in
England. If open squares are "outdoor rooms",
then these provide public "indoor rooms". This
example at Malmesbury dates from c.1500 and
stands at the entry to the precincts of the former
Benedictine Abbey, whose gatehouse can be seen
beyond. Leland wrote that it was "for poor folkes
to stande dry when rayne cummeth". Its function
therefore is really no different from those dreary bus
stands in the Old Market of Beccles (see page 84).
Its location was artistically judged so as to close
the view down the main street in the town.

Malmesbury
Wiltshire

The Market Cross in Malmesbury (seen on the previous page) is, in fact, only a precursor to the main covered public indoor space in the town, the Abbey. While, strictly speaking, church property is private, it is important to remember that where church interiors were publicly accessible, they must have formed an everyday part of the urban experience of town life. Often they were used for markets and assembly as well as for worship, and were effectively the indoor rooms of most towns. This was recognized by Giambattista Nolli, whose celebrated 1748 plan of Rome included the interior layouts of all churches as well as the streets.

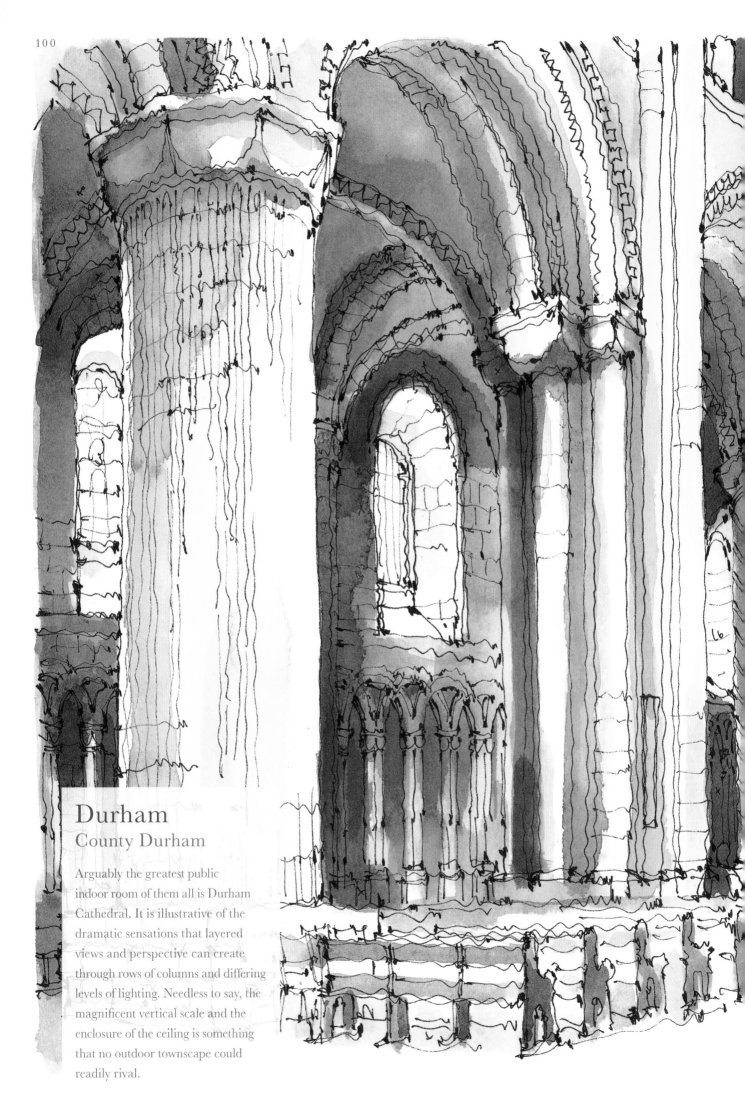

Durham
County Durham

Arguably the greatest public indoor room of them all is Durham Cathedral. It is illustrative of the dramatic sensations that layered views and perspective can create through rows of columns and differing levels of lighting. Needless to say, the magnificent vertical scale and the enclosure of the ceiling is something that no outdoor townscape could readily rival.

Norwich
Norfolk

This view of the south aisle of Norwich Cathedral (left) is enticing because different elements of light and shade draw the eye through a sequence of stone screens to the far distance, similar to the layered views formed in Durham Cathedral (seen on the previous page).

Borough
London

The inspiring layered views of both Durham and Norwich Cathedrals are unexpectedly mirrored in the complex roof canopies of Borough Market in London (right). Here, a medieval pattern of lanes and alleyways is roofed over by nineteenth-century canopies, whose geometry had to contend with overhead Victorian railway arches. The resulting views are chaotic, but rich in character and interest, not least due to the inventive and attractive roof shapes and cast-iron details. Sadly, much of this is soon to be taken down as the nearby railway is to be widened.

Crewe
Cheshire

Of all our indoor public spaces, the railways have provided some of the richest visual scenery. Crewe is
the principle junction of the London-to-Glasgow mainline, and is made up of a collection of structures that
appear to have developed and expanded incrementally. This view occurs where the brickwork walls
(with their attractive multicoloured brick and stone details) are interrupted to allow the passage of an
overhead footbridge, which connects at least 12 platforms and provides a long view through this complex
and unexpectedly picturesque station. Sadly, parts of their structure are now being demolished.

Purley
Surrey

Purley Station is like countless other suburban stations on the railway network, except that all its platform awnings are still remarkably complete. Drawn after dark and long after the commuters have returned to their warm homes, the layered views of platforms look cold, empty, and lonely, extending infinitely into the darkness of the night. The Edwardian "tudorbethan" brickwork of the waiting room adds a homely touch. The awning valance with its wavy edge is like the choppy surface of the sea and is an appropriate detail here, as this route serves much of the south coast. Compare these structures with the impoverished designs of many a recent station and you can see immediately the generosity of vision that we appear to have lost.

King's Cross
London

This view of London King's Cross station shows a very large indoor room, with two framing elements. The first is the roof of the station, which funnels the view towards Scotland and The North. Closer is an iron footbridge, whose delicate lattice pattern is a typical railway design. Here it is furnished with a handsome clock with roman numerals (note the alternative digital version provided underneath). While some might argue that removing this bridge would reveal the structure beyond, this would be a mistake, as in picturesque terms it adds a second frame to the view out of the station itself. Regrettably, this bridge is to be replaced.

King's Cross
London

Turn ninety degrees from the view of King's Cross station on the previous page, and there is a further prospect, this time across the width of the two train sheds. Here, the central spine wall has been pierced with massive arches, some filled in for structural reasons, others left open. These allow sight of the train shed beyond and are rather like a flattened Roman viaduct. The view is further enlivened by another layer of arches on the far wall beyond. One of these is open to the outside world, creating a second double-framed vista.

Gateways

Charing
Kent

Framed views through gateways create the impression that
you are either enclosed, looking out, or excluded and looking
in. The two sensations provide different levels of comfort.
This remarkable barn was once part of a palace belonging to
the Archbishop of Canterbury. Its inclusion here, beyond the
obvious delight of its materials and architectural features, is to
illustrate the framed view through the building, which suggests
a gateway into the farmyard to whatever lies beyond.

Lewes
Sussex

Gateways can be among the
greatest pleasures of our built
environment. The former
gatehouse of Lewes Castle now
consists of only two crumbly flint
arches that span the public road
and frame a glimpse of the high
street beyond. Despite the loss
of the gates, it is still possible to
sense the powerful enclosure of
the former castle precinct.

Snape
Suffolk

A similar effect to that at Lewes occurs at the Snape Maltings in Suffolk where a sequence of structural arches were inserted to buttress the flank walls of the two maltings buildings. These frame a view down the service road and create an almost tunnel-like perspective.

Canterbury
Kent

Here, an incidental gate has been formed for functional reasons: the need
to connect a complex of buildings that accommodated the old city tannery.
The buildings are about as utilitarian as can be, and taken individually, could
never qualify for formal protection. Yet, when collected together, this industrial
townscape is, in its way, a city in microcosm, contained by the river in the
foreground, and with its entrance gateway formed largely of corrugated iron
and rivetted steel. Beyond, the buildings cluster to form a space that still feels
private. It is a remarkably unselfconscious and yet delightfully picturesque
composition, the very qualities that are difficult to preserve when, as here,
the industry has closed and the site is to be redeveloped.

Carmarthen
Carmarthenshire

Traditionally we associate gates with
walled cities, built for defence, and so
by necessity, they are substantial,
powerful, and often intimidating.
Even when this function is removed,
gates emphasize a reassuring sense of
enclosure within and a slightly alienating
exclusion from outside. The gate on the
quayside of Carmarthen frames the dense
and tightly packed historic street of houses
beyond, which contrasts with the empty
quayside of the foreground.

Derry
County Londonderry

Most city gates are no longer active in defence. Until quite
recently, the gates of Derry in Northern Ireland were still
militarized, and there was an unsettling quality about finding
the handsome eighteenth-century Bishop's Gate surrounded by
barbed wire and overshadowed by a modern army control tower.
Despite this daunting arrangement, the framed view of the law
courts and the cathedral spire rising beyond provide clues of the
historic and attractive city that lies within.

NAILORS ROW

Bristol
Gloucestershire

For all the architectural damage inflicted upon Bristol in the last half-century, the city still retains its medieval core. The only surviving city gate is surmounted by the fourteenth-century church of St John on the Wall. The gateway looks positively weighed down by the burden. We are inside the old city here, and the gate's height appears diminished by the falling topography and the high buildings of Broad Street that frame the view. Were we looking uphill to this gate from beyond the arch, the effect would no doubt feel quite different.

Soho
London

The gate across Sherwood Street in Soho was constructed to connect the two halves of the former Regents Palace Hotel. It is an unexpected incident in the heart of London, effectively framing a slot view into Piccadilly Circus in the distance.

thethirdspace

Bath
Somerset

This gateway is in fact a railway bridge, constructed to the designs of
Isambard Kingdom Brunel. It crosses close to the southern edge
of Bath, near its river bridge and the former south gate. As if in response
to the sensitivity of this, the bridge and viaduct were dressed up as a sham
section of a medieval city wall, complete with a sequence of archways
and a turreted gate. The design is more sophisticated than it might first
appear as, looking carefully, it can be seen that the perspective of the three
pedestrian openings all converge on this point. These recall a pattern of
radiating roads that were lost when the buildings around the bridge were
cleared and Brunel's composition was left marooned at the centre of a
modern roundabout. His clever visual conceit was then rudely exposed
and his witty urban intentions were spoiled.

Newcastle upon Tyne
Northumberland

Most framing elements in townscapes occur where
roads and railways pass over bridges that are for the
most part unremarkable. In Newcastle the ground
slopes so deeply to the banks of the River Tyne that
bridges cross this part of the city at a great height.
The approach road to the old A1 Tyne Bridge seems
to float effortlessly over the Victorian cityscape below
and hardly appears to touch the ground. The use of
a sleek painted metal bridge deck with curved
undersides is far preferable to the usual clumsy
and streaky concrete.

Farthing Corner
Kent

Sadly, motorway bridges rarely inspire, but at Farthing Corner on the M2 genuine effort does seem to have been made. The service station was built on two brick bastions that deliberately hug the side of the motorway and are linked by a covered bridge where diners could look down on the speeding cars below. The M2 was one of the first motorways to be built when these roads were deemed new and exciting. Although poorly refitted inside, the structure remains a memorable event on an otherwise monotonously dull road, and forms, effectively, a gateway on this main route to the coast with its ferry connections to Europe and beyond.

Sissinghurst
Kent

Gateways have long been used by private owners, originally
for physical defence, as here at Sissinghurst Castle. Later,
gateways were introduced to frame views in a picturesque way
and to denote the boundaries of gardens and estates. The use of
gateways and clustered buildings, especially those originally
built defensively, can now appear extremely pleasing visually.
This is particularly true here, where there are two gates that are
not aligned and therefore raise further expectation as to what
might exist beyond. This sense of mystery is further enhanced by
a third framing element, the outer yew hedge, which is planted
in such a way as to deny an axial view through both arches.

Stowe
Buckinghamshire

In the eighteenth century, the Buckingham family were amongst the wealthiest landowners in the country, and they surrounded their house at Stowe with a very substantial landholding and remarkable landscaped gardens. By harnessing the maximum possible aesthetic value from the gentle rolling topography, this remarkable vista to the house was framed through a symbolic Corinthian Arch. Railings rather than solid gates were used as it was absolutely essential to preserve the all-important distant view of the house, even when the gates were closed. At this point, the south front of the house is still almost a mile away.

Lamberhurst
Kent

Medieval Scotney Castle was replaced by a new
house in the nineteenth century, but the old fortified
and moated house was left as a "picturesque" ruin in
the gardens. Here, the old gatehouse at the edge of the
moat has lost its arch, and yet even now, the surviving
stonework at the base of the arch still has sufficient
power and presence to denote the sense of a gateway
and successfully frames the view of the old house.

Easton Neston
Northamptonshire

The great architect Nicholas
Hawksmoor understood that forming
a gateway did not necessarily mean an
arch. His masterpiece of 1702 at Easton
Neston is therefore simply framed by
these two magnificently carved stone
piers that originally flanked the original
drive to the west front. As at Scotney
Castle (seen on the previous page), the
sheer mass of masonry is sufficient to
denote the symbolic sense of arrival and
the crossing of a threshold into the private
landscape beyond.

Dalkeith
Midlothian

William Adam's near perfect house of Mavisbank, constructed
in 1723, was one of the first Palladian-styled buildings in
Britain. Sadly it remains a ruin, but its forecourt is still framed
by the flanking pavilions of the house which are connected by
curved screen walls. There is no gateway here (beyond the
sorry security fencing), although perspective ensures that these
lower flanking buildings appear to rise up as you near them,
effectively framing the house as memorably as Hawksmoor's
stone piers at Easton Neston (seen on the previous page). How
tragic and shameful it would be if this house were not saved.

Wembley
London

I must confess to being among those who lament the passing of the
1920s towers at Wembley Stadium. They were just – and only just –
close enough to effectively frame the gateway into the old stadium.
As I pass now on the train, I can see the large space between the new
stadium and the railway lines, and I cannot help but suspect that these
wonderful framing towers could have been retained if the new stadium
had been pushed back and the potentially exhilarating juxtaposition
between old and new appreciated.

Rotherhithe
London

In the last sequence of drawings we saw how gateways can physically
and symbolically denote a sense of inside and outside. The way that
places start and stop is a vital aspect in understanding their form and
overall character. So often towns and villages sprawl ever outwards
with no sense of a properly defined edge. Edge provides an immediate
contrast between built and unbuilt areas, and enables scale to be
appreciated. The best places to experience how appealing this can be
is where the edge is "non-negotiable" due to physical limitations, such as
a riverbank. This drawing, and the one that follows, are a sequence that
connect together to record a short stretch of the Thames river edge in
south-east London prior to redevelopment. Here the workings of
London are built hard up to the riverside, with only a fortuitous
glimpse of St Mary's Rotherhithe Church tower on the right.

Rotherhithe
London

In detail, the density of this walled edge of warehouses is defined
by the consistent use of one material – the brown London stock
brick – and a repetitive pattern of window and door openings
punched through the solid walls. Rather like the main square in
Kirkwall (see page 44), these buildings are generally built
end-on to the river edge to minimize the length of valuable river
frontage taken by each of the individual buildings. The cranes
remind us that this is a working environment, although the gaps
between the buildings betray the changes afoot; this area is now
being converted from warehouses to luxury apartments. Each and
every time one of these warehouses is pulled down, the sense of
a hard edge is diminished.

Embankment
London

Upstream from Rotherhithe (seen on
the previous pages) in central London,
the riverbank was redefined by the
great engineer Joseph Bazalgette.
He made room for a new road,
underground railway, mains sewer,
and a municipal park. It is from this
new park, the Embankment Gardens,
that the line of buildings that once
defined the riverbank now form this
cliff-like edge of grand public edifices.

Liverpool
Lancashire

This same proud early twentieth-century character was even more
strongly expressed in Liverpool, where the important harbour edge
was celebrated by a remarkable group of civic buildings that memorably
marked the historic point of departure for New York and beyond. Sadly,
the clarity of this bold ensemble is now being marred by a rash of new
developments that are rising up behind and in front of this remarkable
group and threatening to blur the eloquence of this unique composition.

Liverpool
Lancashire

Newlyn
Cornwall

On the Cornish coast at Newlyn, buildings have been built up on
a rocky eminence and are robustly faced in rubblestone. Here, the
dense row of houses combines with precipitous topography to create
a similar sense of cliff edge that the buildings alone managed to
achieve in London and Liverpool (seen on the previous pages). The
projecting first floor windows that peer out to sea and give sideways
glances up and down the coast are an especially attractive feature.

Hartlepool
County Durham

Hartlepool was an ancient fishing town that suffered serious bombing in World War I. When it was rebuilt in the 1920s and 1930s, standard developer-designed semi-detached houses were built on the site of the old town. No effort appears to have been made to tailor the design of these houses to their site. They might just have been placed anywhere. Indeed, this style of development is often associated with the urban sprawl that extended around the edges of most British towns in the inter-war period and prompted the establishment of "green belts" around the major cities in the late 1940s. Here, the "semis" appear refreshingly contained behind the medieval town wall, even if apparently oblivious to it. Unlike at Newlyn (seen on the previous page), the buildings are not sufficiently dense to form an "edge" in themselves, and were it not for the medieval town wall, there would be no clear sense of definition to this place, and little to indicate its historic significance except, perhaps, for the presence of Hartlepool's handsome Victorian town hall, which can be seen in the distance.

Sevenoaks
Kent

There are few places left in Britain where the edge of a fully enclosed medieval town can be experienced. It can be imagined at Knole, near Sevenoaks, where the large and rambling ancient house is contained on its north side by an outer and an inner set of walls. Standing in the empty parkland on a cold winter's afternoon, the contrast of the lonely discomfort of the cold field with the cosy-looking and densely packed buildings behind the walls could not be more vividly expressed. Clear edges such as these are much to be preferred to the casual and suburban blur that characterizes the outer reaches of most modern settlements.

Fordcombe
Kent

This view of a house along the road to Fordcombe, close to the Kent–Sussex border, demonstrates how flanking walls can improve the setting of even a fairly ordinary house. Here, the walls curve back graciously to create a generous forecourt to the building. The functional requirement for a wall defining public and private space has been used to architectural advantage, as these walls also form part of the architectural composition of the building and thereby increase the dignity of its setting.

Rye
Sussex

The next sequence of sketches focus on Rye, a small town that neatly encapsulates much of the delight that has been described so far. This first view (left) shows the substantial town gate, framing the street behind, which is enhanced by the topography of the rising hill beyond. This marks the clear edge of the old town. To the right, the arched church buttresses frame a layered view of the buildings beyond, with a narrow passageway formed in between two buildings of different styles but united in their use of similar materials.

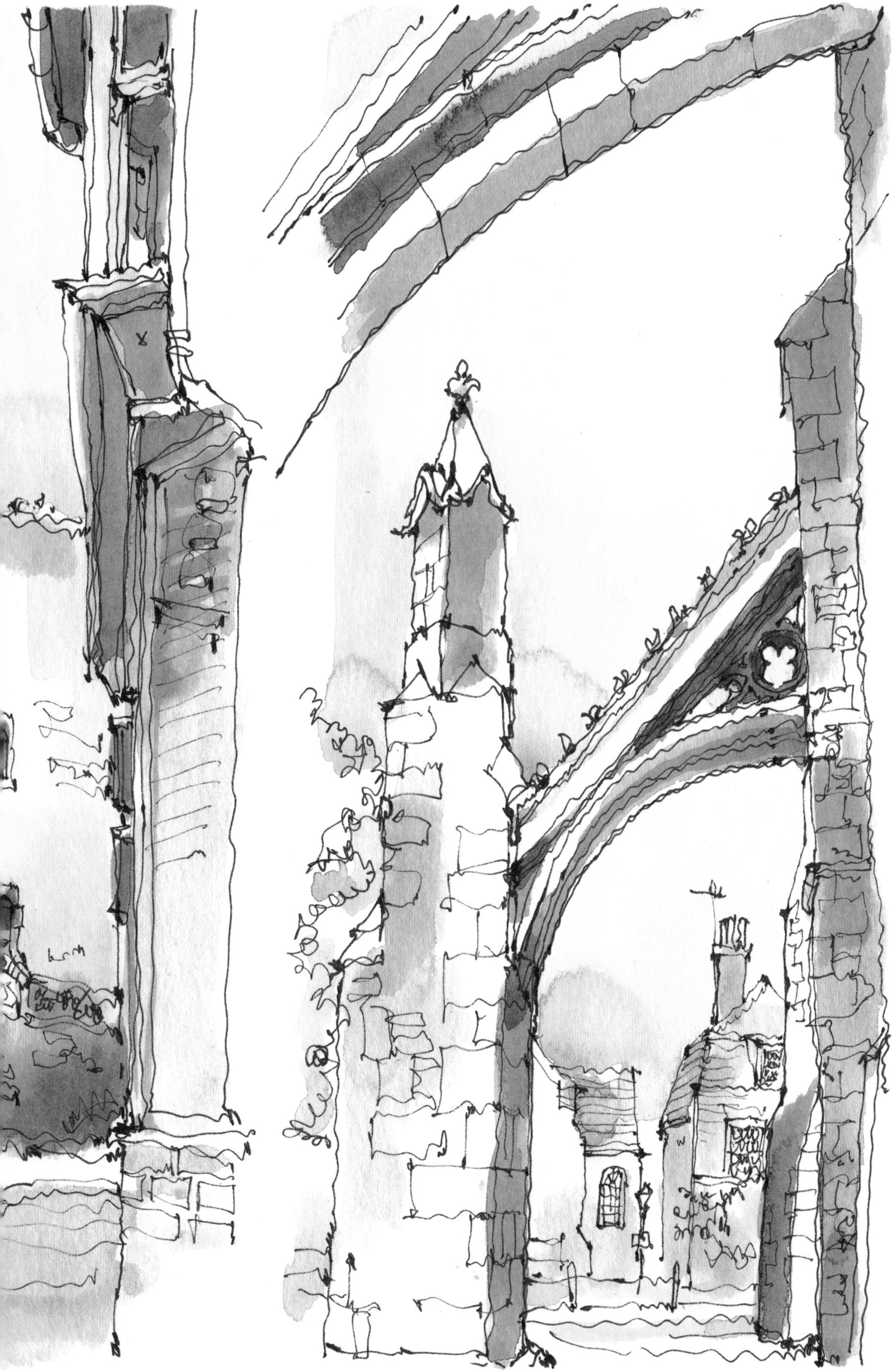

Rye
Sussex

Following on from the drawings on the previous page, these two views are taken from one place. The scene on the left shows an attractively cobbled street rising towards us. The patterns of light and shade and the subtle change in orientation betray the entrance of a side street just down from where we are. At the bottom can be glimpsed the main high street, which runs up from the town gate we saw on the previous page. Rotate ninety degrees (right) and the street has turned a corner to reveal a glimpse of the church (whose flying buttresses we saw on the previous page). The church is partially obscured and framed by flanking buildings that only serve to entice you to explore it further. Here in Rye are many of the secrets of subtle town making that we appear to have forgotten in all too many of our modern housing developments.

Astwood
Buckinghamshire

This next sequence of drawings looks at colour and texture. At some point these cottages were
downgraded to provide farm storage. As Astwood lies on the edge of the limestone belt, both stone
and brick have been used along with timber framing. The bricking up of the old cottage windows
has left this simple building with an almost abstract, decorative quality to its façade. Until recently,
it had been preserved from development by its location under a major pylon route, the wires of
which can be seen on the right.

Texture and colour

Covent Garden
London

There is remarkable richness of texture to a typical
London street, even though the basic palate of local
building materials – brick, paint, and plaster – remains
fairly limited. Tavistock Street in Covent Garden was
blighted by plans for total redevelopment during much
of the 1960s and early 1970s, which effectively protected
it from incremental change during those damaging times.
As a result, it is a finely preserved example of eighteenth-
and nineteenth-century building, with elevations composed
of well-proportioned windows. These openings are all set
deeply into the traditional masonry walls and it is this
depth that creates the regular pattern of shadow and
texture that animates the otherwise fairly simple façades.

King's Norton
Warwickshire

This view depicts what many would
find to be quintessentially "England".
Here, the buildings achieve richness
through their differing textures and
colours. The handsome church spire is
of pinkish sandstone and rises happily
in the backdrop of a timber-beamed
inn with its cream-painted later addition
and attractive bay windows. Quite
apart from the colour and texture, we
seem to have found ourselves in the
world of Miss Marple, cricket, and
cream teas. In fact, this is King's
Norton, which is now a busy suburb
of Birmingham.

Holborn
London

Texture can be especially rewarding when combined with a layering of views. At the northern end of Chancery Lane in London, the muddle of commercial buildings step down to partially reveal the handsome façade of Sir Robert Taylor's "Stone Buildings" of Lincoln's Inn. This building appears rather as the ruins of ancient Rome might be depicted in a Piranesi print – almost subsumed by later structures. There will be those who would want this view to be "opened up" (as with the footbridge at King's Cross station, see page 108), but this would inevitably destroy the enjoyable contrast in scale and texture which contribute to the very quality of the unexpected that makes London so special.

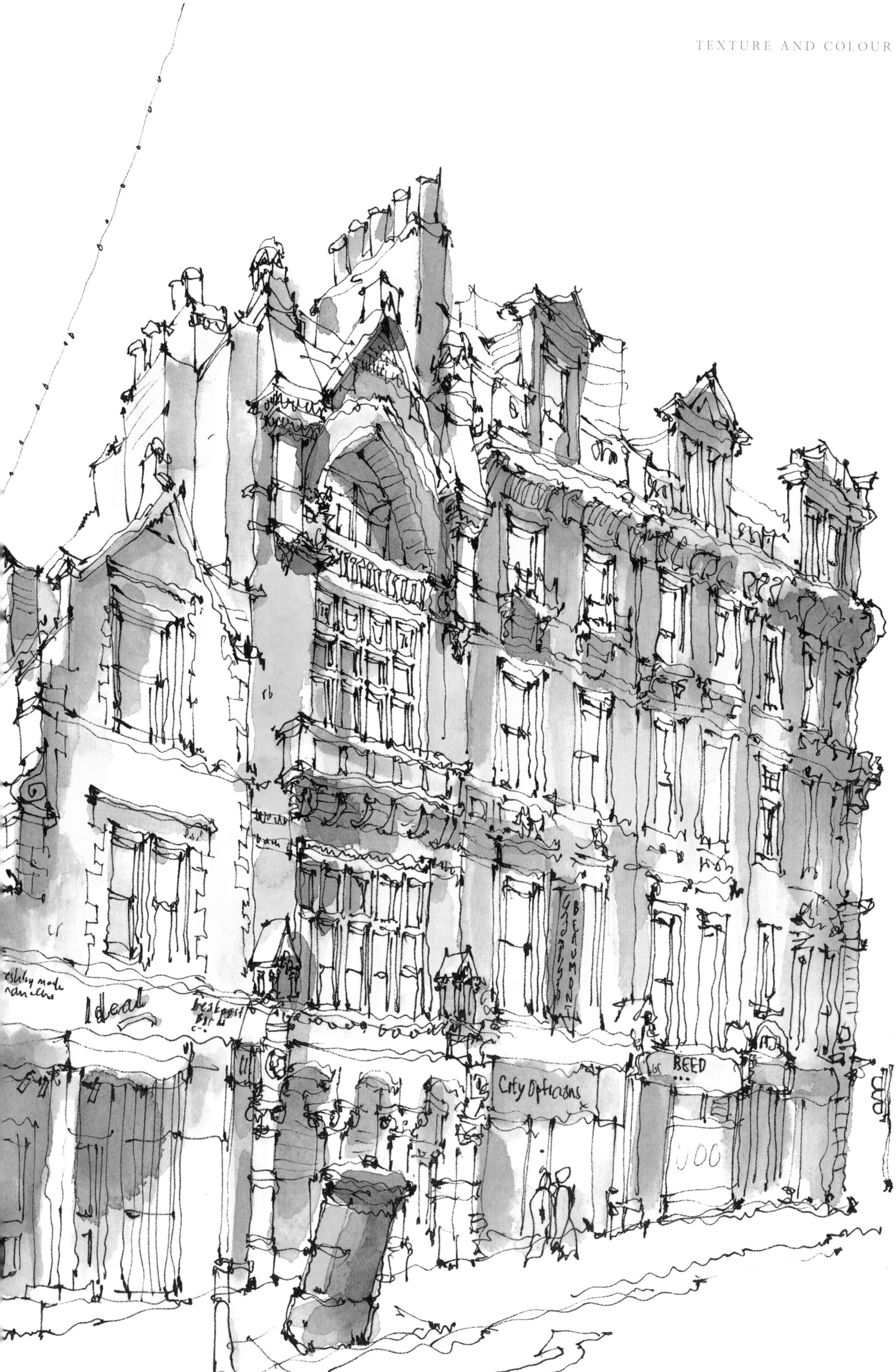
Ideal
City Opticians
BEAUMONT
REED

Westminster
London

I have always appreciated how the rather petite St Margaret's Parish Church, Westminster, was reconstructed c.1482–1523 with such exquisitely rich detail and confidence, as if entirely undaunted by its location in the shadow of medieval Westminster Abbey, which fills most of the view behind it. With the addition in the nineteenth century of Barry and Pugin's Houses of Parliament to the left, this side of Parliament Square reaches a sort of gothic frenzy which must make this one of the most richly textured corners of urban Britain.

Woodbridge
Suffolk

Introducing colour to buildings often requires nerve.
Very often we appear all too satisfied to paint our
ironwork a safe black and our windows a standard white.
Abandonment of these conventions can admittedly lead to
disaster, but more often it creates visual delight, as typified
by this corner building in Woodbridge. It is seemingly a
perfectly ordinary building; indeed, it is almost like a child's
drawing of a house, with its top floor window placed so close
to the upper right-hand corner. It might have remained
happily anonymous, had its owner painted its windows
white and the shop front black. But colour has animated
its façade and emphasized the best of its quirky proportions.

HIGH STREET

CROWN · CROWN

CROWN

KERITAR
BRITISH MADE
VACUUM CLEANERS

Miele

CROWN
VACUUM
CLEANERS
SALES
SPARES
REPAIRS

Tunbridge Wells
Kent

Here colour has a vested interest. It has been deliberately used to encourage our attention towards this shop that appears to sell vacuum cleaners. No need for ugly bright lights or horrid plastic signage here; good old-fashioned yellow paint does the trick perfectly.

Glasgow
Lanarkshire

This building at 85 Buchanan
Street, Glasgow, by the architects
Gillespie Kidd and Coia (1968–
70) was clad in copper which
remains brown on the protected
side, but has turned green on the
principal façade. The colour and
texture is as rich and evocative of
its time as the nineteenth-century
building next door.

Strand
London

In London, much of the city's colour is provided by the vivid red of the buses, one of which is parked here next to the church of St Mary-le-Strand, a masterpiece by James Gibbs of 1714–23. There seems to be a natural synergy between the bulging masonry of the church apse and the curvaceous roof of the bus.

Strand
London

If the observation made on the previous page about the positive
colour of London's red buses needed further emphasis, then this
view of the Strand make the point. The Strand was once the
principle link between the old cities of London and Westminster.
The church in the distance is St Mary-le-Strand (seen on
the previous page) with the tower of Sir Christopher Wren's
St Clement Danes church beyond. This view seems to convey the
very essence of London, as each building takes its place in
the background. No jarring high-rise office building has been
allowed to damage the balance – yet. The recent replacement
of the well-proportioned double-decker "Routemaster" buses
with the long and boxy European "bendy buses" is a matter of
regret only partially mitigated by the continuation of the red livery.

Edinburgh
Midlothian

Along with red buses and letter boxes, that other great provider of colour to the often dour streets of Britain is the red telephone box, whose multi-paned windows seem to fit perfectly into almost any location. We have already seen them on the village streets of Sussex (see page 24), Yorkshire (see page 34), and Orkney (see pages 44 and 58). Here four sit happily among the Old Town tenements of the Edinburgh Royal Mile, adding a cheerful dose of colour to an otherwise grey scene.

A matter of scale

Victoria
London

As we have already seen, scale is a subjective thing and is often related to perspective and proximity. Here London buses appear to overshadow Victoria station. Such contrasts of scale can be unexpectedly exhilarating as the next sequence of drawings seeks to illustrate.

Holcombe Rogus
Devon

Scale and perpective can be harnessed to produce unexpected and stimulating visual effects. When seen from a certain place, the slender towers of the house at Holcombe Rogus rise dramatically above the circular dovecote and the tower of the village church beyond. All of these come together in this particular view, but from anywhere else, this relationship would not be immediately apparent.

Hailsham
Sussex

Herstmonceux Castle was built after 1440.
Its turrets have faceted sides that capture
the light differently and exaggerate their
height. From this location, the towers
cluster to create a dramatic vertical
grouping; a sort of Tudor Manhattan.

Ipswich
Suffolk

Ipswich is an ancient county town whose docks have suffered decades of decline. In this view, the jolly red-brick tower of the nineteenth-century Custom House is seen against a higher and almost windowless grain store, which is made of grey concrete. The grain store might be considered intrusive because of its bulk and height, and yet with its vertically ribbed concrete walls and lack of surface decoration, it contrasts unexpectedly in this view with the decorative architecture of the tower. Beyond, two of the town's medieval church towers close the street vista.

Westminster
London

The visual effect of sequential
towers found on the previous
page at Herstmonceux Castle is
seen again here at the top of
Victoria Street in London, with
the towers of Westminster Abbey,
St Margaret's Parish Church
(see page 168), and the Houses
of Parliament. The end of the
Victorian building in the
foreground, with its pair of
handsome chimneys, provides
the perfect vertical emphasis,
as does the slender monument
that partially obscures
St Stephen's Tower.

Brighton
Sussex

The church of St Bartholomew in Brighton is an enormous building that dates from 1872–74 and towers over the small houses built next to it. In fact, it is the smallness of the houses that appears to dramatize the large scale of the church. This visual effect would be lost if the small houses were removed.

Harrogate
Yorkshire

In Harrogate contrast is achieved between the war memorial and the surrounding buildings, but more through colour and texture rather than height. Against the buildings in the background, the stone obelisk looks full and massive. This effect is enhanced by the memorial's plain and white Portland stone surface, which contrasts with the dark, sooty, and richly detailed sandstone of the buildings surrounding it. It manages to hold its own, even next to the taller buildings on the right. If any of these buildings were changed, this brilliantly controlled contrast of colour and texture could be diminished.

Embankment
London

Scale can be created as much by the control of empty spaces between buildings, as by the buildings themselves. The sequence of buildings facing Embankment Gardens (see page 146) is interrupted by an ancient alleyway that rises up the old river bank to connect to the Strand (see page 176), where a further wall of buildings is sliced to allow a view towards the Covent Garden market building. This is sufficiently low to keep the view open to the sky, enabling the narrow slot of space to be read, making the buildings either side look especially tall.

Carmarthen
Carmarthenshire

A further medieval street whose restricted width has been exaggerated occurs in Carmarthen where the monumental classical law courts face the imposing medieval castle. With such a tight space between the two structures, this feels like an urban "stand off", which would not have conveyed a fraction of the drama had the street in between been any wider.

Dagenham
London

The potential power of thin slots of space, such as those demonstrated by the views from London's Embankment Gardens and Carmarthen on the previous pages, were exploited to enhance the sense of height, and therefore civic grandeur, of the portico of Dagenham Town Hall in East London by E Bury Weber in 1936 (left). He must have deliberately distorted this slot of space to achieve a sense of scale that would otherwise not have been available in this generally low-rise neighbourhood.

Marylebone
London

A stranger slot of space occurred for a short while in 2005 under the tower of the former Abbey National Building on Baker Street (right), which was left propped up with scaffolding, as the building beneath it was completely demolished. The tower was presumably considered a skyline feature that could not be lost. The sliver of sky that is visible under the tower, between the steel supports, is unexpected and dramatic indeed.

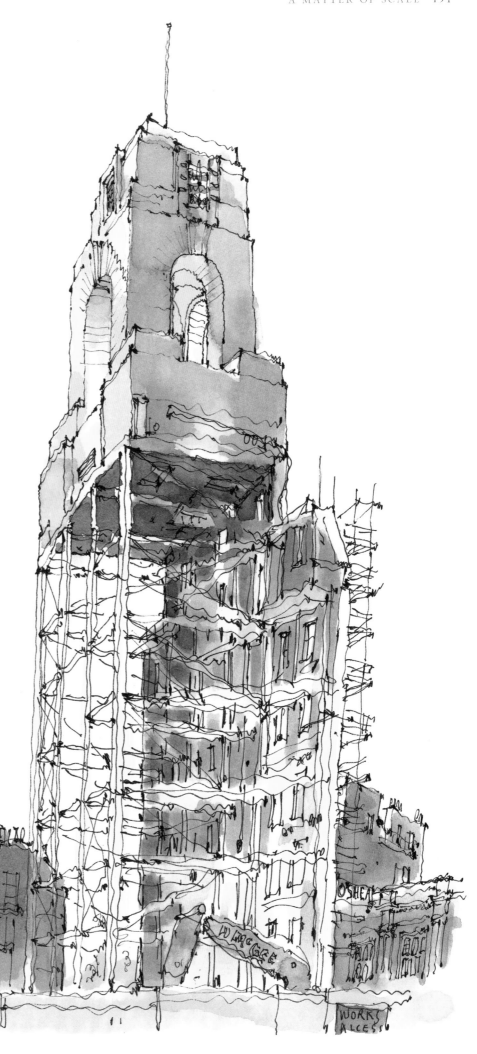

Norwich
Norfolk

Tall buildings rising above the general townscape inevitably create a wide visual impact, which can be shaped and manipulated to create a skyline. These can be beautiful and evocative if the buildings that appear on the skyline retain a vertical emphasis and a balanced scale. But skylines are surprisingly delicate and have proved very easy to spoil. In its day, Norwich had more churches than any other city outside of London. It still benefits from a rich skyline of clustered church towers, each of which was carefully designed to create an attractive profile when seen from afar. During the 1930s a new town hall was added, whose taller and brick-built campanile was an entirely fitting and sensitive addition to this skyline. Happily absent from this view is the intrusive block of a multi-storey car park, from which this scene was drawn, and which has sadly marred the composition of the Norwich skyline from many parts of the city.

Liverpool
Lancashire

The skyline of Liverpool is one of the most memorable of any British city and demonstrates how a handful of tall, vertical structures can create a strong urban identity. Surprisingly, this skyline has been made almost entirely by twentieth-century buildings: the Anglican cathedral (Sir Giles Gilbert Scott, 1902) is on the extreme left, the Roman Catholic Cathedral (Sir Frederick Gibberd, 1962) is in the centre, and to the right are the twin towers of the Royal Liver Friendly Society building (1908). Even the 1960s rotating restaurant on the extreme right-hand side (now a radio station) has a "pop-icon" appeal. It seems that all of these buildings were carefully designed to ensure that their relationship with the sky was considered and that their silhouettes had grace. The delicate balance achieved here at Liverpool is now very vulnerable because of new high-rise apartment building proposals, whose bulky forms could intrude into this composition and rob the city of one of its finest features.

Ipswich
Suffolk

Ipswich, like Norwich (see page 192), was a
wealthy town in the Middle Ages with
numerous church towers. Here, however, the
mix has gained a collection of large industrial
concrete grain stores (see also page 184). The
shape, size, density, and raw quality of these
buildings establish an alternative skyline order.
But again, the emphasis and proportion remains
vertical and they are sufficiently clustered
together so as not to destroy entirely the skyline
of the ancient church towers. Perhaps this is
because these grain stores are largely windowless.
They have become "background" buildings and
act as a foil for the more delicate textures of the
church towers. This balance would change if
the grain stores were to be replaced by new
buildings of a more assertive and "iconic" design.

City of London
London

St Paul's Cathedral in the City of London
has long been overshadowed by high-rise
office buildings. Much of the time, however,
the cathedral is framed by cranes working
on the seemingly endless redevelopment
of the commercial office sites that surround
it. The cranes unwittingly frame the dome
and create unexpected visual effects, such
as this view, which occurred during the
redevelopment of Paternoster Square,
immediately north of the cathedral.

Battersea
London

The inside of the gutted shell of the former
powerstation at Battersea is the best – and
least expected – place from which to
appreciate the magnificence of its former
chimneys. Due to the demolition of the
building they once framed, the chimneys
are now seen to rise to a tremendous height.

Salisbury
Wiltshire

It has sometimes been argued that if people had rallied against high buildings in the Middle Ages then Salisbury Cathedral spire (left) might never have been constructed. The argument is often used in defence of new high-rise office and apartment blocks. If all high-rise buildings were as elegantly proportioned and finely crafted as Salisbury Cathedral spire – admittedly a challenging feat – then we might feel more tempted to rejoice in them.

Birmingham
Warwickshire

There is a coincidental similarity of massing between this view of New Street, Birmingham and Salisbury (left). Both compositions have a tall element in the centre, with medium-height blocks on either side. However, the hard-edged, flat rooftops of the Birmingham buildings have less grace than those that meet the sky with a point.

Westminster
London

This scene was the only one drawn specifically for this book. It shows the
River Thames in London, taken from Hungerford Railway Bridge. The
buildings on the right are of a low scale that makes the river seem wide
and impressive. Next are the Houses of Parliament, with their romantic,
pinacled skyline, which looks good in any light. Until 1963 Parliament
used to star centre stage in this wonderful urban show. But then, one
further building – the Millbank Tower – was added. Whatever its merits,
the Millbank Tower seems the wrong building in the wrong place, and
if you were to place your hand over this building on the drawing, you
could see how the view is improved without it. Inexplicably, the
Millbank Tower is now a listed building and has consequently acted
as a catalyst for more new high-rise buildings nearby that, when
constructed, will ruin this view in perpetuity.

Leeds
Yorkshire

This final section of drawings gathers together curiosities and frustrations in our everyday surroundings. One building that creates delight is this mill in Leeds. It dates from 1838 and is a fairly loose reinterpretation of an Egyptian temple. The building is made out of the local Yorkshire sandstone and is found on an ordinary back street next to various other industrial structures with little or no architectural pretension. How refreshing to commission and construct something of such originality, simply for its architectural pleasure. Presumably it was an expression of pride by its owner. Above all, this is a fun building and should act as an inspiration to others in our pragmatic, cost-engineered and all too often banal world.

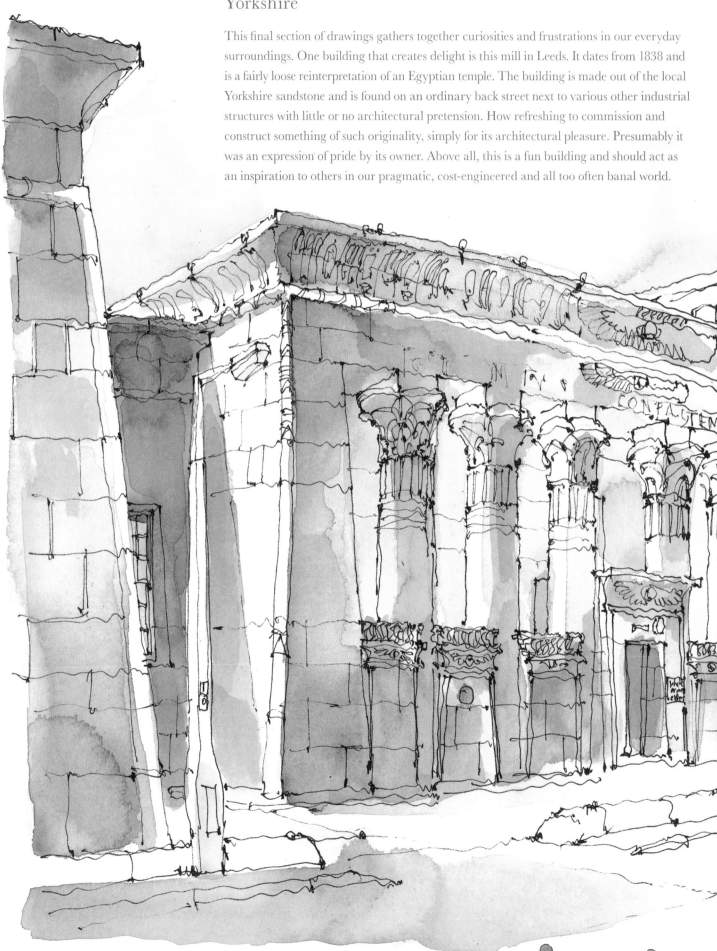

Alderley Edge
Cheshire

Garages these days are often no more than standard kit structures and the same
everywhere. Alderley Edge has long been a wealthy commuter area for Manchester,
and is an obvious location for a car showroom designed to attract attention. Rather
like the M2 service station (see page 128), this highly original 1960s car showroom
building conveys the fresh excitement of the car that we now all take for granted.
With its futuristic appearance it makes a striking contrast with Alderley Edge's
traditional Victorian parish church, visible on the right.

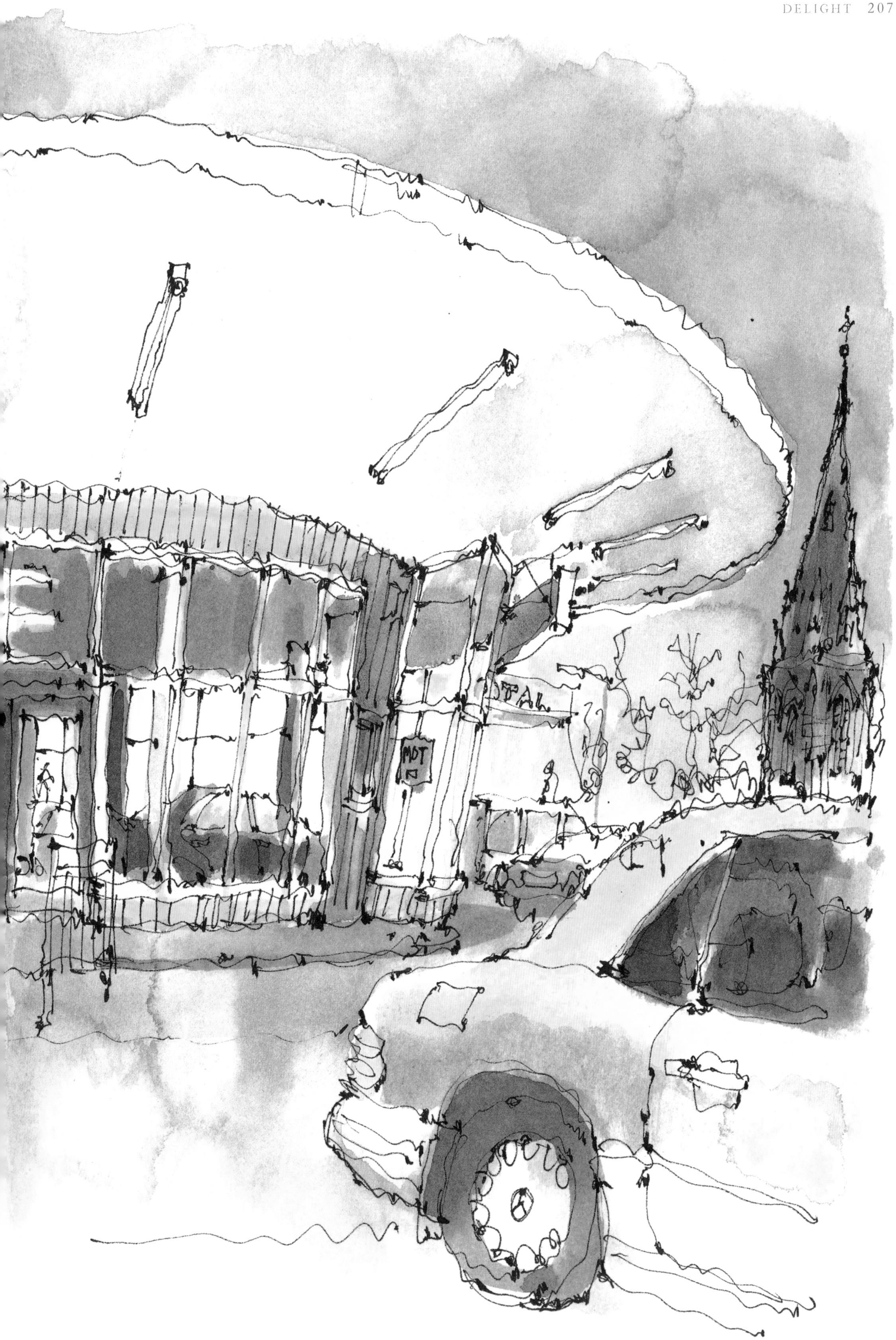
MOT

Bangor
County Down

For reasons unknown, this dovecote is perched on open arches at the centre of the very large stable yard behind Clandeboye House, only seven miles from central Belfast. And yet, visually it is an act of genius, providing focus to this irregular open area. Note the corbelling that widens the upper storey of the building, a curious detail that hardly saves much space below. If space were short, why build it here at all?

Sheerness
Kent

World War II brought about some of the most curious and striking structures
ever built. This strange trilogy of gun-encasement buildings once protected
the former boatyard at Sheerness on the Isle of Sheppey from enemy attack.
I wonder why each one was made to look so different. Two have round bases, one
a square base. One has a hexagonal top. The centre one has a slate roof, cosy
red-brick chimney stack, and sash windows but the same aggressive slot opening
and concrete walling as its neighbours. With their peculiar shapes and strange
forms, they have long been abandoned. They linger on like strange, fossilized
beasts from an alien civilization and I, for one, hope that they can be preserved.

Hove
Sussex

Street lighting, as we have already seen, can add significantly to the beauty and delight of a place. This was understood by the Victorians, who added handsome street furniture to many towns. By the sea especially, an extensive range of cast-iron awnings, shelters, lamps, and railings were developed and introduced. The seafront of Hove and Brighton was one of the visually richest because of its sheer length (about four miles). The lamps along the sea front at Hove were different from those at Brighton and had cast-iron brackets featuring sea birds in oak-tree foliage, a symbolic representation of this coastal part of Sussex.

SOLD

Hove
Sussex

This second view of Hove (seen also on the previous page)
is taken where the Victorian development gives way to
buildings of the Edwardian era and the twentieth century.
Even here the two lamps nearest to us have a grace and
character that is sadly lacking in those standard motorway
products that can be seen looming beyond. Tragically, all
of these lamps (and also those on the previous page) are
in the process of being replaced with modern fixtures.
Hove's urban elegance is being pillaged, and its distinctive
character reduced as a result.

Longtown
Cumberland

We have already seen how traffic engineering can spoil a historic place, such as at the old market in Beccles (see page 84). But the triumph of traffic engineers in their insertion of ugly street lighting into virtually every town across the land seems to have passed largely unnoticed. Longtown is a single-street border town with attractive rendered houses whose scale has been utterly overwhelmed by the towering street lighting, which might well have come off a slip road to the M6 motorway. Removal of these lamps and their replacement with lower lighting, perhaps more closely spaced if demanded in the cause of safety, would enhance this town significantly.

Ashbourne
Derbyshire

Writing in *Buildings of England: Derbyshire*, Sir Nikolaus Pevsner noted of Ashbourne that "Church Street is one of the finest streets of Derbyshire. It has a large variety of excellent houses and whole stretches without anything that could jar." This was presumably written before the introduction of the dreadful "off-the-peg" trunk-road lamp posts that so visibly intrude into the area of sky that should be left clear. Can such ugliness really be justified in the cause of "health and safety"?

Worcester
Worcestershire

The final sketches of this book are reserved for the diminishing delight of
railway paraphernalia. Manually controlled railways signals, such as these at
Worcester Shrub Hill (left), may not be an obvious object to draw, but they are
fun, colourful, and evocative of childhood. They are also fast approaching
extinction as the railways move to computer technology.

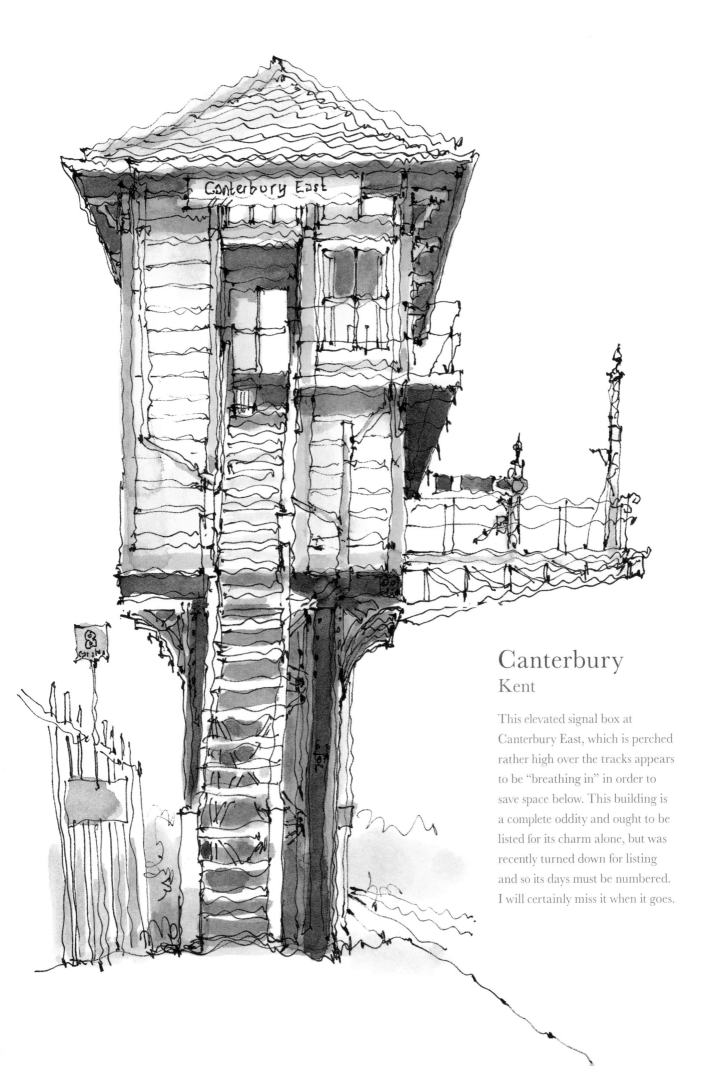

Canterbury
Kent

This elevated signal box at
Canterbury East, which is perched
rather high over the tracks appears
to be "breathing in" in order to
save space below. This building is
a complete oddity and ought to be
listed for its charm alone, but was
recently turned down for listing
and so its days must be numbered.
I will certainly miss it when it goes.

Lincoln
Lincolnshire

On Lincoln High Street there is the improbable combination of a railway signal box and the old stone conduit from the medieval whitefriars, which was relocated into the churchyard of St Mary-le-Wigford in 1540. The two buildings stand side by side and are obviously of totally different ages, materials, and construction, and yet together they form a dynamic grouping that returns us to the starting point of this book; the lessons learnt from those simple clustered farmyard buildings (see pages 14 to 25). On their own, either building would be attractive, but together they become a more interesting and unexpected entity. Regrettably, the signal box is now scheduled for removal. I would rather it were kept, as I enjoy the juxtaposition of the railway age next to an earlier architectural order. Obviously not everything can be saved, but if the drawings in this book encourage more recognition of the delight that we all have around us, then half the battle may yet be won.

Index

Ptolemy Dean

Ptolemy Dean trained as an architect at the Bartlett in London and the University of Edinburgh and now runs his own architectural practice in London, which specializes in the repair of historic buildings and the creation of new buildings in a historic context. New buildings designed at Southwark Cathedral with Richard Griffiths won national RIBA and Civic Trust Awards and projects at Farnham Church and the restoration of garden structures at Temple Guiting, with landscape architect Jinny Blom, have also won awards.

Ptolemy Dean appeared as a historic buildings adviser in the popular BBC Two programme *Restoration* and presented BBC Four's *The Perfect Village*. He has written two books on Sir John Soane, one of which was shortlisted for the 2007 Sir Nikolaus Pevsner RIBA award.

He currently serves on the London Advisory Committee of English Heritage, the Architectural Panel of the National Trust, and the Salisbury Cathedral Fabric Advisory Committee. He lives with his wife and two children in a semi-derelict farmyard in East Sussex, which he hopes one day to restore.

Acknowledgements

This book owes a great deal to all those who have waited for me over the years to make "just a quick sketch", in particular Michael Beanland, Duncan Woodburn, and Chris Fogarty. The programme directors at Endemol UK always permitted sketches during the *Restoration* film shoots, and Marianne Sühr was notably patient. Will Palin and Richard Pollard made helpful comments on the introduction, while the drawing of the skyline of Liverpool was only made possible by the kindness of Peter Rawlinson, who opened the doors to the tower of Edge Hill Church. Members of my office in London have assisted in numerous ways, particularly my associates Udo Heinrich and Kirstie Robinson. And then there is Stephanie Jackson of DK, who had the courage and vision to commission this book over gin and tonic on various trains to Tunbridge Wells. Elizabeth Watson nobly transferred the various scrawls into reality. Finally, I must thank my long-suffering wife Charlotte, without whom all might seem pointless.

Dorling Kindersley would like to thank Susie Adams, Adam Brackenbury, Joern Kroeger, and Natascha Sturny for their work on the images and May Corfield for proofreading.

UNITED KINGDOM
FEATURED LOCATIONS:

N

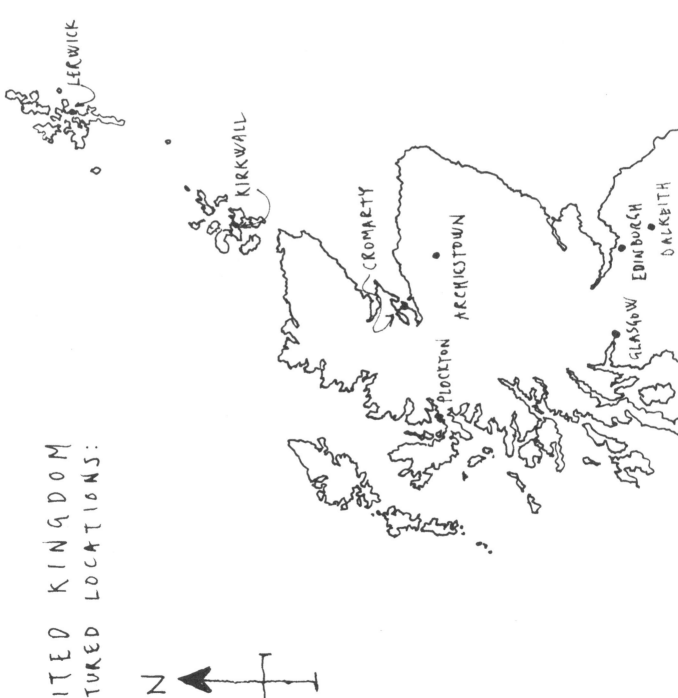

LERWICK

KIRKWALL

CROMARTY

ARCHIESTOWN

PLOCKTON

GLASGOW

EDINBURGH

DALKEITH